Growing Up in Coal Country

Growing Up in Coal Country

Susan Campbell Bartoletti

Houghton Mifflin Company Boston

For information about this and other Houghton Mifflin trade and reference books and
multimedia products, visit The Bookstore at Houghton Mifflin on the World Wide Web at
http://www.hmco.com/trade/.

Book design by Susan Mallory Sherman, Ars Agassiz, Cambridge, Massachusetts
The text of this book is set in 13 point Monotype Baskerville, for the Macintosh.

Manufactured in the United States of America
CRW 10 9 8 7 6 5

Library of Congress Cataloging-in-Publication Data

Bartoletti, Susan Campbell.
Growing up in coal country / by Susan Campbell Bartoletti.
p. cm.
Summary: Describes what life was like, especially for children, in coal mines and mining
towns in the nineteenth and twentieth centuries.
RNF ISBN 0-395-77847-6 PAP ISBN 0-395-97914-5
1. Children — Employment — Pennsylvania — History — Juvenile literature. 2. Coal
miners—Pennsylvania — History — Juvenile literature. 3. Immigrants — Pennsylvania —
History—Juvenile literature. 4. Anthracite coal industry — Pennsylvania — History —
Juvenile literature. 5. Coal mines and mining — Pennsylvania — History — Juvenile
literature. [1. Coal miners. 2. Coal mines and mining.] I. Title.
HD6247.M6152U63 1996
331.3 ' 822334 ' 09748 — dc20
96-3142 CIP AC

For Sonny and Rita Bartoletti,
with love.

Contents

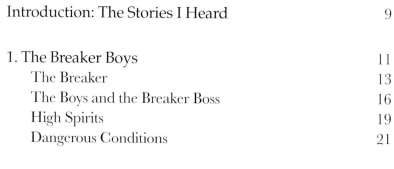

Massimino and Pearl Santarelli on their wedding day, October 22, 1924.
Family photograph, Joseph Bartoletti

Introduction

The Stories I Heard

At our dinner table, my husband's grandparents, Massimino and Pearl Santarelli, often told stories about what it was like to grow up in coal country.

I heard how Massimino came to the United States from Italy as a young boy; how he quit school to work in the coal breaker when he was eleven; how he was kicked by a mule; how he dug coal on his hands and knees from chambers too low to stand in; and how his uncle, his nephew, and his best friend were all killed in mining accidents.

I heard how Pearl quit school in first grade to help her mother; how her father was injured in a mining accident; how she married Massimino when she was thirteen and had her first baby at fourteen; how she baked fifteen loaves of bread each week; how one year she burned all the Easter breads; and how, after mining all day, Massimino spent his evenings building her a house.

Massimino's and Pearl's stories fascinated me, and I wanted to hear more. I took a tape recorder and sought out stories from other relatives. I placed notices in newspapers and church bulletins and found other people who invited me into their living rooms and told me their stories.

I read old mining inspection records, newspapers, magazines, and books. In museum archives, I searched through boxes of interview transcripts and listened to recorded interviews. I studied old photographs.

Slowly, I was able to piece together what life was like for the children of coal country in northeastern Pennsylvania—children who lived, worked, and played nearly one hundred years ago. This is their story.

1 The Breaker Boys

At the age of eight, I left school and was given a job in the mines. I found it pretty hard getting out of bed at five-thirty every morning. The first two months, the road to work wasn't bad, but with the coming of snow, I found that I was much too small to make my way to work alone. Many times I was forced to wait by the side of the road for an older man to help me through the snow. Often I was lifted to the shoulders of some fellow miner and carried right to the colliery.

— *Anonymous*

SHAMOKIN, PA. ENTERPRISE COLLIERY.

Copyrighted by

Myron Thomas, Shamokin, Pa.

The coal breaker, the tall building where coal was broken and sorted for market, shadowed the rest of the surface operation of the colliery.
Paul Thomas Studio,
Shamokin, Pennsylvania

In coal country, the workdays began before dawn. A thin icy blast from the breaker whistle roused sleeping children from the beds that they shared with their brothers and sisters. They ran downstairs to warm up by the kitchen coal stove. Their mother was busy stoking the coal, making breakfast, and packing tin lunch pails.

Fathers and sons ate quickly, then got ready for work. The men dressed in coveralls and rubber boots. The boys pulled on caps and overcoats and laced up hobnailed

12

boots. They grabbed their lunch pails and headed down the dark streets leading to the mines.

The young boys worked in the coal breaker, the tall gloomy structure where coal was broken and sorted. Each day, the breaker boys met and walked to the breaker together, laughing and joking about some prank that may have been played on another boy or on the boss. The youngest breaker boys, sometimes five or six years old, were accompanied by their mothers to and from work, even though by law they were much too young.

According to an 1885 law, boys had to be at least twelve to work in the coal breakers and fourteen to work inside the mines. A 1902 law later raised the age to work in the breakers to fourteen. But parents and coal operators found it easy to get around the law in Pennsylvania, which had no compulsory registration of births. When a father wished to get his son a job, he obtained an "age blank" or certificate from a mine inspector, filled in the age he wanted his son to be, and for a twenty-five-cent fee had the certificate notarized. This way young boys were passed off as "small for fourteen."

The Breaker

The inside of a breaker was a large, noisy room. It had high walls and a flight of narrow steps that climbed past blackened wooden beams and grimy windows. Long iron chutes ran from the top of the breaker to the floor.

The boys took their seats on pine boards lying astride

13

the chutes. Because not everything that came out of the mines was coal—it was a mixture of coal, rock, slate, and other refuse—it was up to the breaker boys to pick out the refuse, or culm, as the coal flowed down the long iron chutes.

As each full coal car emerged from the mine, it was pulled to the top of the breaker by a long steel cable. There, a man threw a lever, the car tipped, and the coal rushed out onto a shaking machine, which pushed the coal

toward the long chutes that ran from the top of the breaker to the bottom.

As the coal streamed down the chutes toward the boys,
it spewed black clouds of coal dust, steam, and smoke,
which settled over the boys like a blanket and turned their
faces and clothing coal-black.

To keep from inhaling the dust, the boys wore handkerchiefs over their mouths. Behind the handkerchiefs, their
jaws worked on wads of tobacco that they chewed to keep
their mouths moist. "Smoking was not allowed," said
James Sullivan. "Chewing tobacco was supposed to prevent the breaker dust from going down your throat."

The boys used their feet to stop the flow of coal. They
picked out pieces of slate and rock from the chutes, then
lifted their feet so that the coal continued to the next boy.
The slate and rock were tossed into another chute, which
emptied into cars that were dumped at the culm banks.
The culm banks grew into large, coarse gray mountains
that surrounded the colliery and the mine workers' homes.
The clean coal continued on into railroad cars, ready for
market.

*After the coal cars emerged from the
mine, they were hauled to the top of
the breaker.*
Canal Museum at Hugh Moore Park,
Easton, Pennsylvania

All around the boys, deafening machinery crushed and
separated tons of coal into various sizes, ranging from rice
to pea to stone to egg. When the breaker was running at
full capacity, work began at seven in the morning and did
not end until six or six-thirty at night. Since the boys
weren't allowed to nail backrests to their seats, their backs
ached from sitting in a hunched position all day.

15

At the top of the breaker, the full cars were tipped, and the largest pieces of slate were picked out before the coal was crushed and sent down the chutes to the boys.

Canal Museum at Hugh Moore Park, Easton, Pennsylvania

The bosses also forbade the boys to wear gloves, even in the coldest weather, because they impaired their sense of touch and finger movement. "If we were discovered wearing gloves," remembered one breaker boy, "the boss would strike our knuckles with a long stick he carried."

As a result, for the first few weeks, the sulfur "muck" on the coal irritated the boys' skin and caused their fingers to swell, crack open, and bleed. This painful condition was called "red tips."

After the boys had worked two or three weeks, their fingers hardened and there were no more red tips. In the meantime, however, mothers applied goose grease to their sons' fingers each night.

The Boys and the Breaker Boss

The breaker boss circulated around the boys. He carried a stick or broom and watched for the boys who daydreamed, dozed, talked, turned their heads, or worked too slowly. "If the boss caught you slipping up and letting slate come down," said Joseph Miliauskas, "you'd get it in your back with the broom." Some bosses kicked the boys in the ribs or rapped them across the back of the neck or stomped on their fingers with hobnailed boots.

If the breaker boys thought they were being treated unfairly, they often retaliated by teasing or annoying the breaker boss. They whipped pieces of slate or rock at him when his back was turned. Or they threw pieces of slate or board into the breaker machinery, causing it to break down. While the machinery was being repaired, the boys ran wild, playing games and having fun.

Up to ten million tons of culm were dumped from a breaker every year.
Pennsylvania Historical and Museum Commission, Division of Archives and Manuscripts

Sometimes the boys protested by swarming out of the breaker and refusing to work. A breaker-boy strike effectively shut down the entire colliery because all operations halted if the breaker wasn't working. To force the boys back to work, the bosses often "whipped them in" with actual whips. The boys' fathers—who were also losing money—often helped the bosses.

At a Pottsville breaker, the bosses blocked the doorway to prevent the protesting boys from escaping. Several boys scrambled to the top of the rafters and kicked clouds of coal dust down on the bosses' heads. While the bosses were stooped over, coughing and spitting coal dust, the boys ran out the door.

The boys were forbidden to wear gloves because it impaired their sense of touch. Before their skin toughened, their fingers swelled, cracked open, and bled.

George Bretz Collection, Albin O. Kuhn Library, University of Maryland, Baltimore County

At a Moosic breaker, the boys plotted to get even with a particularly cruel boss. Instead of going to work one July morning, they went swimming. When their boss found them at the swimming hole, two boys rushed him from behind and knocked him into the water. The rest of the boys joined in and gave their boss several good dunkings before he was rescued by the superintendent and another foreman.

18

Sometimes the boys weren't even sure why they were striking. When one boy asked, "What are we striking for?" another boy responded, "I don't know, but I'll be damned if we'll give up until we get it."

High Spirits

Even though the work was hard, the breaker boys remained bright, cheerful, and full of tricks. It was too loud to talk to other boys, but Carlo Brunori described how the boys where he worked communicated when the foreman's back was turned. "The boys made an alphabet with their fingers. They had a sign for every letter and they would make words. They were experts at it. Their fingers would fly, telling all their friends about the dances and everything they were doing."

A new boy was a likely target for pranks and practical jokes. "The older boys would grab hold of him," said Carlo Brunori, "and pull his pants down and initiate him with axle grease all over his body. One thing you couldn't get away with was being a snitcher—a squealer. The other boys would tie your street clothes in a knot and nail them to the wall or fill your gloves with sand. Or they might do something to your food. They would nail your dinner pail to the floor, and you wouldn't know until you picked it up and only half was in your hand and half was still nailed to the floor."

Richard Owens told how the boys would carry grease and a bucket of coal dust to the top of the breaker.

"They'd make a ball out of the grease and put it in the bucket of coal dust. Then they'd throw the greaseball down on you. It would smother you with all the dust. If the ball hit your back, it would hurt. Your back was hurting anyhow, because you'd been in the same position for eight hours. If we ever got the chance, we'd get even with the boy who dropped the greaseball. It was tit for tat."

The boys also delighted in pelting well-dressed visitors with stones when the boss's back was turned.

At noontime, the breaker whistle blew, signaling time for lunch. The breaker shut down, and the boys flocked together to compare lunches and to play games like baseball, football, and tag. At some break-ers, the boys sneaked their lunches early so they would have extra time to play.

"We knew every hole in the break-er," said Joseph Miliauskas. "And we'd hide and go through it in com-plete darkness. We'd go over the machinery and around it. You'd get to know it because everything stops during the lunch hour. We'd get to know it like a bunch of rats."

At noontime, the breaker boys gathered for football and other games.
Wyoming Historical and Geological Society

Jere Stanton remembered the pitched battles the boys fought at noontime: "We stoned one another. Some of the boys would run to the shops and get nuts and other pieces of iron for missiles. When the whistle blew for us to return to the breaker, we did so and the fight was over."

Dangerous Conditions

The breaker boys' high spirits and natural curiosity some-times led to disaster. Fingers were caught in conveyers and cut off. Small boys fell down the long coal chutes and became buried and smothered in the coal.

One ballad tells about a small boy nicknamed Mickey Pick-Slate, who was a breaker boy in the Audenreid break-er near Hazleton. One day, Mickey fell into the crusher rolls and was ground up with the coal. His mother, who had walked him to and from work each day, lost her mind.

This boy oiled the shafting and other moving pieces of breaker machinery.
Pennsylvania Historical and Museum Commission, Division of Archives and Manuscripts

Each day, she continued to wait at the breaker for him, scanning the sooty face of each young boy as he walked past, looking for her Mickey.

> *Mickey Pick-Slate, early and late,*
> *That was this poor little breaker boy's fate;*
> *A poor simple woman at the breaker still waits,*
> *To take home her Mickey Pick-Slate.*

Manus McHugh was another boy who lost his life in the breaker. His job was to oil the breaker machinery. At noontime one day he was in a hurry because he wanted to get outside to play with the others. Rather than take the time to shut the machinery down, he attempted to oil it while it was still in motion. His arm got caught in the gears and he became hopelessly entangled.

After an investigation of McHugh's death, a 1903 report stated, "Boys will be boys and must play, unless they are held under by strict discipline." But other than that, no changes were made to make conditions safer for the boys.

2 Nippers, Spraggers, and Mule Drivers

My first day in the mines was down the Number One shaft at Bear Creek Colliery. The shaft was 321 feet deep. I don't think I'll ever forget the terrible sensation I had while descending that morning. I was so dizzy that when I was halfway down, I thought I was going up.

— *Joseph McCormick*

At the beginning of the shift, mine workers received safety lamps from the fire boss. The lamps were used to check for dangerous gases.

Dave Krewson, Clarks Summit, Pennsylvania

Boys who survived working in the breakers went on to other jobs. Most had envied the older boys who worked underground in the mines, and they longed to join them. There, they would be free of the breaker, its noisy machinery, and its foremen. As Joseph Miliauskas, a former breaker boy, said, "When I got down into the mines, that was paradise."

26

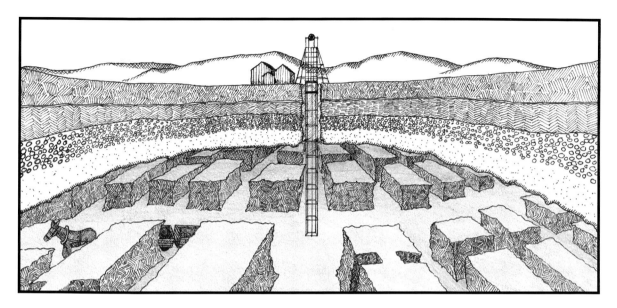

The Mines

To descend into the mines, the workers either rode the man-trip cars that rolled down the slope like a roller coaster or squeezed into an elevator-like cage that dropped down the shaft.

At the bottom, sometimes twelve hundred feet or more below the surface, the boys and men stepped out. Total darkness surrounded the workers, except where the greasy yellow light shone from their pit lamps. The workers tramped to the whitewashed underground office built into the rock. The office was well lit and warm compared to the rest of the mine, where the air was damp and the temperature remained a constant forty-eight degrees year-round.

Each worker hung his identification tag on a pegboard

A mine was laid out like a vast underground city. Wide roads, or chutes, were driven off both sides of the main road, called the gangway. Smaller passages, called monkeyheads, ran parallel to the main gangway and connected the chutes. Some mines had over ten miles of tunnels winding through the underground.

At the beginning of each workday, the fire boss checked for dangerous gases.

outside the office. The tags let the mine operators know each worker's location in the mine—a necessary precaution in case of a disaster such as a cave-in or an explosion.

The miners checked for any notes left by the fire boss about the condition of their work area. The fire boss was the first person in the mine each day. As early as four or five o'clock in the morning, while all of coal country was still asleep, he made his rounds throughout the chambers, checking thoroughly for dangerous gases and unstable roofs. He wrote his notes on a slate and hung the slate at the underground office.

If the slate was clean, meaning the fire boss had found the chamber safe, the workers headed down the gangway. Lunch pails banged against knees, and gravel crunched beneath boots. The flames from carbide lamps fluttered like bright birds, casting eerie shadows on the walls.

Farther past the mule barn, which was home for the mules that worked in the mines, the gangway branched off into different passageways. The passageways had fancy names like "Primrose" and "Peach Orchard." Each level of the mine was like a vast underground city with as many as ten miles of entangled tunnels leading to the various work chambers.

Nippers

The nipper or door tender was the youngest of the underground boys, usually eleven to thirteen years old. His job was to open and close the heavy wooden doors that were constructed across the gangways or headings of the mine.

The doors were an important part of the mine's ventilation. Above ground, huge fans forced fresh air into the mines. When the doors were closed, the air hit the doors and turned into the tunnels and chambers where the miners were working. The flow of air also pushed out dangerous gases, like methane, so they didn't build up in pockets and explode.

As the nipper sat on his bench outside the door, he listened for the rumbling approach of empty cars headed

When Willie heard an approaching mine car, he opened the door for the mule and its driver.

into the chambers or full cars coming out. Sometimes mules pulled the cars through the doorway; other times, in sloped areas, the cars rolled by gravity alone. When the nipper heard the cars, he opened the door to let them pass through, then made sure the door swung tightly closed behind them.

It was a long day for the nipper, who became bored sitting all alone in the dark, with only a little glow from his carbide lamp. Usually, the lamp didn't throw enough light to read by, so the nipper looked for other ways to amuse himself and stay awake at his post.

To pass the time, the nipper whittled long pieces of wood into sprags or fed crusts of bread to the huge rats that watched with red eyes. Some nippers, like Patrick McNulty, trapped the rats: "I amused myself for hours trapping the rats. I would make a trap out of a powder tin with some paper or other light material for a top, on which I placed a piece of bread or other food. When the rat climbed onto the light cover for the food, it would fall into the can, and a heavier lid would clamp down so it could not get out. Sometimes when I got two rats in the can, they would fight."

The nipper knew that falling asleep could be disastrous. If the mine doors weren't open, the racing mine cars, which weighed about four tons when full, crashed into the doors. In 1903, a young nipper who fell asleep beside the gangway jumped up when he heard the approaching mine cars. He ran to throw open the doors, but it was too late. The mine cars struck and killed him.

Joseph Miliauskas remembered the day he fell asleep and the mine cars crashed into the unopened doors: "I had stretched out on my bench and put my lamp alongside me. . . . I must have dozed off because the next thing I knew I heard a bang. I jumped up. The bib to my coveralls was on fire, and there was my door on top of a loaded car." No one was hurt, and Joseph was lucky not to lose his job.

The darkness and solitude bred courage and responsibility in the boys. Ominous creaks, groans, and trickling sounds forewarned that a roof was "working," which meant the rock was loose overhead and in danger of collapse. If a roof was working in a gangway or heading, the nipper was usually the first to hear the telltale sounds and could run to warn the others.

The spraggers in this group proudly displayed their wooden sprags.
Lewis Hine Collection, Albin O. Kuhn Library, University of Maryland, Baltimore County

Spraggers

Only the fastest and most agile boys were picked to be spraggers, the boys who controlled the speed of the mine cars as they rolled down the slope. Spraggers usually worked in pairs. Each boy had about twenty or thirty long pieces of wood called sprags. As the train of mine cars rolled downhill—sometimes as many as eight at one time—the spraggers ran alongside the cars and jabbed the sprags into the wheels of each car. The sprags worked as brakes, locking the wheels in place and slowing the cars down.

Spragging was dangerous work. The boys dodged low ceilings and passageways that narrowed without warning to clearances of only several inches. "A spragger had to be good," said Patrick McNulty. "He became such an expert at putting the sprags in on the fly that he would not miss a wheel. . . . At times, though, the spraggers' hands or fingers got too close to the car and instantly became wedged and sheared off."

If the wheels weren't spragged properly, the cars flew out of control. Often they toppled or jumped the track and crashed into the mine wall, sometimes injuring the spragger.

Because miners were paid by the weight of the cars they filled, they lost money for any coal that was spilled— even if it wasn't their fault. To ensure that the spraggers

Wooden sprags were inserted into the wheels to brake the mine car.

Dave Krewson, Clarks Summit, Pennsylvania

33

Mule drivers became so skilled with their black snake whips that they could extinguish the flame on a lantern without upsetting the lantern.

Applied Arts Publishers

and mule drivers did a good job, the miners often gave them tobacco and invited them to their homes on Saturday night for dinner and beer. As one boy said, "It was to the miner's advantage to keep on the right side of the driver and spragger."

The boys loved the danger and excitement of their work. At least they weren't hunched over long chutes of coal or perched on benches outside the gangway doors. Here, in the miles of tunnels, they even found opportunity to have fun. "We'd stand on the bumper and ride the cars down the slope," said Richard Owens. "It was pretty lively going down that way. Of course, the bosses didn't like it."

The bosses didn't like it because nearly forty percent of fatal accidents happened when the boys riding the cars were struck by a low ceiling or when they fell off and were run over or dragged by the cars. Many boys had arms or legs severed when their limbs got caught in the wheels. If a boy survived the accident, he sometimes died later from infection.

Mule Drivers

The most glorious job of all was that of the mule driver, for it offered danger, excitement, and—best of all—freedom to move about the mines.

The mule driver, usually a boy in his early teens, traveled from one work chamber to the next, coupling the full cars together and leaving an empty car to be filled. A boy started out with one mule, then worked his way up to a six-

mule team. When he was able to drive six mules, he was given a man's wages and earned the respect of all the workers and bosses. "He drove mules in the mines" was all the recommendation a driver needed for a job later in life.

Because of the narrow passageways, the mules were harnessed in tandem, one behind the other. Drivers chose

The driver sat or stood on the front car bumper. He didn't use reins to direct the mule; he used only his voice.

Pennsylvania Historical and Museum Commission, Bureau of Historic Sites and Museums, Anthracite Museum Complex

During an average day, each mule hauled about one hundred tons of coal. A full car weighed about four tons.

Pennsylvania Historical and Museum Commission, Bureau of Historic Sites and Museums, Anthracite Museum Complex

the smartest mule as the leader, and the leader was fitted with a miner's lamp attached to its harness or its collar.

The driver sat or stood on the front car bumper, where he used only his voice to guide the mules. He yelled "gee" for a right turn, "wah-haw" for a left turn, "whoa" for stop, and "giddap" for go. If the mules were stubborn and refused to move, he cracked a warning in the air with his long, braided black leather snake whip.

Most foremen didn't allow the boys to carry watches, because they wanted their workers to concentrate on the number of cars, not the time. "I had thirteen places to take care of with one mule," said Robert Reid. "I had to get six cars from every chamber. If I accomplished this by quitting time, all was well and good. If not, I had to stay until

36

the work was done, and I received no extra pay for the additional time required."

To entertain themselves and their mules, the mule drivers often made up songs. One popular song was "My Sweetheart's the Mule in the Mines."

My sweetheart's the mule in the mines,
I drive her without reins or lines,
On the bumper I sit,
I chew and I spit,
All over my sweetheart's behind.

If there was a lull in the work, the drivers practiced their skill with the whip. They set their mine lamps a short distance away, and with a crack of the whip, they tried to extinguish the flame without upsetting the lamp.

Mule drivers were considered the most notorious pranksters. "If you weren't looking," said Emil Ermert, "the mule boy would go through your lunch pail and eat all your goodies before you got back [from opening the doors]. I learned to eat my pie or cake first before somebody else got it."

The Courage of Martin Crahan

During the West Pittston mine shaft fire in 1871, Martin Crahan, a twelve-year-old mule driver, refused to ride the cage to safety because he knew there were nineteen miners who needed to be warned of the fire.

Martin found the miners, told them about the fire, then ran back to the elevator cage. It was too late; the cage had already been destroyed. Realizing there was no hope for rescue, he found his way back to the miners through the smoke and flames. In the meantime, the miners had built a barricade in hope of keeping out the poisonous fumes. Martin begged the miners to let him in, but they refused because that would also let the gases in.

Rather than die alone, Martin headed for the mule stable. He found his mule, scratched a final message to his family, then died next to his mule. The other miners died, too.

William McKinney and His Mule

On Easter Monday in 1879, mule driver William McKinney told his mother not to pack much lunch for him because he planned to be home early. He sneaked extra lumps of sugar into his pocket for his mule, Harry.

At work, as William and Harry plodded along the gangway, William saw rats heading up the slope. A few seconds later he heard a terrible crash, and a gust of wind and dust pushed the mule back and knocked William off the mine car.

A large cave-in had crushed the gangway and the airway. "I thought of the men inside," said William. "I knew the air was shut off and that some would be burned or blown up if we did not go in to warn them. So I gave Harry a jab in the ribs with the sprag, and away we went."

William found two gangs of men and warned them, and then another cave-in occurred. "It was like a big thunderstorm, with timbers crackling and splitting until broken. . . . We were trapped. Everything around us was sealed tight. Harry and I were alone with seven other men."

For three days, William and the men waited for rescue. As they sat, they talked about family and friends. Their lunches were gone, and all they had were two gallons of oil and four safety lamps.

By the fourth day, with no sign of help, there was still nothing to eat. "When I looked at the others," said William, "their eyes seemed to be bulging out of their heads, and they looked wild. . . . Finally, one of the men looked at Harry and said, 'I think if I had a piece of that mule, I'd eat it.'" After much thought, William said, "I'll bring the mule here, but I won't kill it. One of you will have to."

As William held Harry by the bridle, Harry sniffed William's pockets for sugar. Through tears, William told the mule, "Harry, I guess I'll never give you any more sugar, because I'm going to take you out to be made into meat so these men can live."

Harry was killed, cut up, and fried on the lid of a lunch pail. After nine days, rescuers found the entombed men.

When William came out, his mother was overjoyed to see him. She gave him the new suit she had planned to bury him in.

3 Mules and Rats

My first day, I asked the stableman who was going to show me how to handle the mule and do the job. He informed me that if I wished any information on the subject, I should ask the mule. He told me to watch the mule and learn something. I led the mule to the rock tunnel, where a line of empty cars waited. As we approached, he drew up before the last car and almost told me to hook a car [onto him]. Sure enough, my mule knew the job from A to Z, and he was a very good teacher.

— Anonymous

Most boys treated their mules like pets, but some drivers were cruel. One Wilkes-Barre driver was given a jail sentence for beating his mule when it refused to move.

Postcard Collection of Charles Kumpas, Clarks Summit, Pennsylvania

The Sweethearts of the Mine

The sure-footed, sturdy "sweethearts" of the mine combined the size and power of their mother, the horse, with the perseverance and sure-footedness of their father, the donkey.

The compact build of the mules was ideal for working in narrow passageways and under low roofs. As they plodded along the gangways, their ears functioned like antennae against the roof, allowing the mules to judge when to

42

drop their heads and avoid injury if the ceiling suddenly lowered. Eventually, the tips of their ears wore off.

In large mines, the mules seldom left their underground homes.
Postcard Collection of Charles Kumpas, Clarks Summit, Pennsylvania

The mules lived deep in the mines, in stables cut out of rock and other materials. Usually the stables were located near the cage, which made it easier to transport refuse, food, water, and other supplies.

For most of the boys, the mules became pets, and the boys took good care of them. They cleaned the mule stables daily, sprinkled lime over the straw several times a week, filled the feed boxes, and made sure the trough held fresh water. Each morning they currycombed their mules and checked the fit of the harnesses so they wouldn't cause shoulder galls, or sores, as the mules pulled the heavy mine cars.

In addition to the oats, corn, alfalfa, cake meal, and salt that the mules were fed, the boys brought apples, carrots, and other goodies to work, and even asked their mothers to pack extra sandwiches. When this wasn't enough, the mules simply helped themselves to whatever the boys had—hard-boiled eggs, pork chops, bread and jam, banana and orange peels, egg shells, bread crusts, tin lunch pails, and parts of the boys' clothing.

In smaller mines, the mules went home at the end of the workday as well.

Paul Thomas Studio, Shamokin, Pennsylvania

The boys also shared plugs of tobacco with their mules. Like true friends, the boys offered their mules the first bite, then jammed the rest of the tobacco into their own mouths. Some mules became so addicted to tobacco that they refused to work until they were given their share.

The mules were crafty, and in order to be a driver, a boy had to be at least as smart as the mule. There was often a struggle to determine who would be master. Sometimes the boy won; often the mule was winner.

The mine workers learned to depend upon the mule's good memory for direction and instinct for survival. They claimed that the mules knew their way throughout the winding tunnels better than anyone. If the mine workers lost their way, they unharnessed the mules and followed them to safety.

After one deadly explosion deep in the mines, no miner was left to warn the others of the danger. A small black mule that survived the blast ran from level to level until it reached the surface. When the surface workers noticed the mule's singed body, they realized that disaster had struck and a fire raged below.

44

Still, the mule's intelligence frustrated the drivers. The mules knew how many cars they were supposed to pull, and if a driver sneaked on another car, the mules wouldn't budge until the car was removed. The mules also knew instinctively when it was quitting time, even though no whistle could be heard in the mines. At quitting time, the mules simply halted wherever they happened to be. No amount of coaxing or bullying seemed to budge a mule that had made up its mind.

"One mule would lie down and wouldn't get up," said Victor Mickatavage, who began working with his father at age eleven and eventually became a mine inspector. "The only way to get him up was to pour some water in the mule's ear. And boy, did that mule jump up. Whoever had that mule had to have a container of water with him" when the mule lay down on the job.

Some angry drivers twisted a stubborn mule's ears, beat him with a stick, or singed his belly with the carbide light. But mules had excellent memories. Even after weeks had passed, they remembered the boys who were mean to them. A well-timed kick in the belly or the seat of the pants proved fatal to many boys.

"[The mules] would trample you or kick you," remembered Emil Ermert, who tended the door. "Anything at all, they'd get even. A six-mule team in a tandem would

Often, the mules knew their way about the winding tunnels better than any mine worker.

Lewis Hine Collection, Albin O. Kuhn Library, University of Maryland, Baltimore County

45

The cage lowered mules and their feed into the mines and hoisted refuse from the underground stable.

Wyoming Historical and Geological Society

stop in the gangway—the mules would never stand in a straight line. They would be staggered, this way and that. If you wanted to pass them, you had to walk past either their back or front end. Either way, you were likely to get kicked or bit or squeezed into the mine rib. It was very scary."

Victor Mickatavage explained how the boys avoided

getting squeezed against a mine rib or wall. "The driver carried a sprag, and he'd set one end against the wall and the other against the mule's rib. That way, the mule could squeeze and push all he wanted and it wouldn't hurt the boy."

With some particularly nasty mules, there was no telling when they would get the urge to take a bite out of their keepers. "Once I happened to have a little spare time after cleaning out the stable," said one stablehand. "So I decided to take a little sleep. How long I slept, I don't know, but I was awakened by a sharp pain in my left hand. I jumped up but found [my left hand] was held firmly in the jaws of a huge mule. Two fingers were missing. For this experience I was discharged by the boss, and all hope of becoming a mule driver was gone."

Some people believed that the mules went blind from working in darkness and dim light for so many years, but at least one study says this wasn't true. Fifty thousand mules were brought to the surface during the long strike of 1925. All were examined, and not one mule was blind.

In fact, many mine workers believed that the animals were treated better than the boys and men. Mules were expensive to replace, whereas workers could be replaced by hiring someone else. In one instance, during a mine fire, the cage was being used to evacuate men and boys to the surface. When the coal operators ordered that one mule be loaded onto each cage, the men protested and finally the order was withdrawn. In at least two mining districts,

Cats were sometimes brought into the mines to keep the rats away.
Dave Krewson, Clarks Summit, Pennsylvania

whenever a mule was lost in an accident, the loss was made up by raising the price on food and supplies at the company store.

When the mules died, their bodies were hoisted to the surface and buried in the mule cemetery. Otherwise, live mules seldom left the mines or their underground mule stables, unless it was a holiday or the coal company was predicting a long strike. When the mules were brought to the surface, they trembled in the sunlight at first, but soon cavorted in the grass and fresh air. It then became nearly impossible to force them back down into the mines. In 1966, a law was finally passed that made it illegal to keep mules in the mines.

Harbingers of Bad Fortune

Huge colonies of rats also lived in the mines. They entered the mines by stowing away in the mules' hay. Once there, they thrived and grew to enormous size. Some miners claimed they saw rats as big as cats.

"There was hardly any sound at all in the mines," said Joseph O'Boyle, "except a miner at work with his pick and drill in some nearby chamber. Most of the time the silence was so heavy you could almost feel its weight. Occasionally a rat would squeal and the intense silence would be broken. Then we would smile."

Like the mules, the rats matched wits with the mine workers. They invaded the mules' feed boxes, and when the mules pushed them away with their noses, the rats

48

Colonies of rats thrived in the mines; as many as two hundred rats lived together in one colony.
National Archives

attacked them. "I've seen lots of mules who were ripped open from rats," recalled a fire boss. Stablehands were kept busy driving the rats away.

Although the rats ate the mules' feed, they also begged crusts from the miners. "I'd be eating my lunch," said Samuel Wentovich, "and [the rats] would be standing up on their hind legs like squirrels, looking at us. If I had any food left over in my pail, I used to dump it right on the side for the rats. They'd grab the crust and run away." The rats, the miners claimed, ate anything—even the waste from the miners and the mules.

More shameless rats didn't beg: they knocked over full lunch pails. When the lid fell off, the rats helped themselves to the entire lunch. According to the mine workers, larger

Stablehands were kept busy driving rats away from the mules' feed.
National Archives

rats simply stole the entire lunch pail by wrapping their tail around the handle, then dragging it off to some dark corner. "You had to keep your lunch close by," said Carlo Brunori. "They'd take anything—even your clothes if you left them lying around. They'd drag them away and hide them."

Eric McKeever remembered what happened to his grandfather's false teeth: "Pappy got ready to eat his sardine sandwich one Friday and removed his false teeth. A large rat leaped up, grabbed the teeth, and ran off with them. While Pap pursued the rat, another rat ate his sandwich. He never did get his false teeth back, nor did he get lunch that day."

Still, the mine workers respected the rats and believed it was bad luck to harm them, because someday a rat might save a mine worker's life. They believed that the rats' keen hearing could detect crackling and splintering sounds that the human ear couldn't. Therefore, if the rats suddenly panicked and headed up the slopes, the mine workers quickly followed, for they believed that the rats always abandoned the mines if a cave-in was imminent or if poisonous gases were present.

Joseph O'Boyle remembered the day he saw a pack of rats scurrying past him, heading up the slopes: "It could only mean one thing: a major fall of rock. We dropped everything and followed the rats. [Behind me] I heard a deafening crash of timber and rock. When the fall had worked itself out, we went back to examine the damage. The machinery, tools, and everything were buried under tons of rock."

Still another miner credited a rat's thievery with saving his life. One day, the miner set a piece of pie on his lunch pail lid. A rat came by and snatched the lid. The miner chased the rat as it scurried down the gangway, still carrying the lid and pie. He retrieved the lid and the pie, and he sat down in his lunch spot to eat it. The rat sneaked by and stole the lid and pie again. The irate miner gave another chase, and while he was chasing the rat, the roof caved in at the very spot where he had been sitting. The rat, the miner claimed, sensed the impending cave-in and stole the pie to safely lure him from danger.

The coal mine operators tried their best to convince the workers that rats were not truly harbingers of bad fortune. But the miners could not be persuaded.

4 The Miner and His Butty

I know about the mines from the talk at our dinner table when I was growing up. The miners and butties had to dig so much coal to fill that car and there couldn't be any rock in it or they'd be penalized. They worked in the water below the roof where it was very dangerous and they'd be on their hands and knees. When my father and brothers came home from work, they were very dirty. Their clothes were heavy with water and dirt and we would have to wash them. My father thought nothing of working in the mines because it was the only work he knew how to do. He never complained. He just did it. But I knew if I ever had a son, I didn't want him to work in the mines.

— Mary Fanucci

Pennsylvania Historical and Museum Commission, Division of Archives and Manuscripts

Nippers, spraggers, and mule drivers envied the miners and the laborers, whose strength was measured in coal. "It always fascinated me to watch the guys going up the chutes and blasting the coal," said Howard Smith. "And it bugged me that I had to stay in the gangway. It wasn't too long before I went up the chutes, too."

The Work Begins

Each miner hired his own butty, or helper. As the workers headed to their assigned areas, they carried all the tools and supplies they needed—picks, shovels, bars, drills, powder, fuses, axes, and lumber.

After the explosive was set, the miners and butties crawled to a safe place to wait until the dust had settled and the smoke had cleared.

Dave Krewson, Clarks Summit, Pennsylvania

54

In their chamber, they inspected the area carefully for poisonous gases or an unstable roof—just as the fire boss had done earlier. Before lanterns were used to check for carbon monoxide, some mine workers used canaries. The miner brought the caged canary into the mines. If the canary became panicky, the miner knew that carbon monoxide was present and further ventilation was necessary.

Rescuers sometimes used a caged canary to be sure the air was safe.
National Archives

If the roof had loose pieces of rock, the miner and his butty knocked the pieces down. If the roof needed propping, they hammered new timbers in place. Once the area was secure, the real work began.

From the miner, the young butty learned the craft of mining. He brought the miner his tools and supplies, filled his lamp with oil, and did odd jobs. Then he watched as the miner drilled holes into the coal seams, tamped in the explosives, and fired them from a safe distance. After the smoke had cleared, the butty shoveled the chunks of fallen coal into the mine cars.

Most butties looked forward to the day when they could become skilled miners. "I like to work in the mines," said William Jones, a former butty. "It's the only work I ever did. I was born with a shovel in my hand, and I will die, I guess, with one in my hand."

Often the butty was a son, nephew, or other relative of the miner. In some mines, however, relatives weren't

Expert timbering supported the roof after the coal was blasted.

Paul Thomas Studio, Shamokin, Pennsylvania

allowed to work together. "I worked alongside my father for six months," said Carlo Brunori. "And then one day the foreman said, 'I have to take you away from your father, because if there's an accident, two will be lost in the same family.'"

Some miners worked in groups of four—two miners and two butties. "When you work in two-man teams," said Howard Smith, "it's good if you have someone who can shovel lefty and the other righty. . . . You would work together and the work would go faster that way."

Sometimes the teams didn't even speak the same language. Many bosses thought the workers worked harder if they couldn't communicate. As they worked, many mine workers taught the immigrants English. Others taught them profanities. The immigrants then tried out their new words on the bosses—with unexpected results.

The Freedom of the Mines

In spite of poor wages, backbreaking work, and dangerous conditions, mine workers found freedom in their chambers far below the earth's surface—a freedom that could not be found in any above-ground factory or mill. This freedom resulted partly from the fact that the mines contained so many miles of tunnels.

Because of the distance and the length of time it took to get from chamber to chamber, the foreman came by only once a week or so to check on the workers. This left the miner to work on his own and, in essence, be his own boss.

The miner bought his own tools, lights, fuses, blasting powder, and blacksmithing, and he paid his butty, whom he had hired himself. Since the miner took care of his own expenses, he grew to resent anyone else telling him what to do in his chamber—even if the chamber and its coal were owned by the coal company. "Why should a boss tell me where to put in my shots when I pay for the powder?" said one miner.

The miners taught their young butties the ways of the mines. "Here comes the boss. Don't work. Always sit when the boss is around," they would whisper when the foreman came by. No factory or mill wanted to hire former mine workers because they said that the mine workers' rebellious natures made them unfit for factory and mill work.

Deep in the mines, no mine worker needed a breaker whistle or clock to tell him when his workday was done. He worked until "full coal" was reached. For most miners, full coal meant five or six four-ton cars per day. When enough coal had been blasted to fill his quota, the miner packed up his tools and quit for the day, leaving his butty to fill the

The miners averaged five full cars a day.
Library of Congress

Lunches usually consisted of a sandwich or two, pie or cake, and fruit.
Library of Congress

cars while he went fishing or blueberry picking.

Some miners reached their quotas by lunchtime. This annoyed the foreman, who thought the miners should stay and blast more coal. But as one miner put it, "A man ought to know when he's tired." More likely, he felt he had worked enough for the day.

Working Conditions

Still, the foreman tried to impose discipline on the mine workers. One way was to assign a miner to a poor work area. The work conditions varied throughout the mines, and rebellious workers were sometimes assigned to areas where water collected knee-deep or the coal seams were narrow, forcing them to crawl on their hands and knees in "monkey holes." Or they had to work where roofs were unstable and required wooden props that the miners had to buy themselves. These conditions determined how difficult the mining was and how much the miner earned.

"This was not the grand job it had seemed to be," remembered Thomas Miller. "If we hit a good place, where the vein was thick and the coal easy to mine, we made money. However, it wasn't unusual for us to go into the hole for the amount of supplies purchased from the store."

Miners resented being assigned to bad spots. When one miner found the water in his chamber was too deep, he told the foreman he deserved more money for working in

When the mine roof and walls settled, the timbers were squeezed.

Canal Museum at Hugh Moore Park, Easton, Pennsylvania

such a wet spot. The foreman refused, saying the water wasn't all that bad. Infuriated, the miner proved his point by picking up the foreman and throwing him in the water to show just how deep it was.

As time went on, the coal operators looked for other ways to get more work out of the miners. One way was to

Each mine car had to be topped. Some operators claimed that dishonest mine workers purposely covered the car floors with rubble instead of coal.
Wyoming Historical and Geological Society

require that each three-ton car be "topped" or heaped with coal. Extra boards framed the top of each car so that it could hold more coal. The additional boards added an extra ton.

"When the cars came out [of the mines]," said Richard Owens, "the boss would rest his elbow on the car to make sure the top of the coal reached the tip of his fingers. If the car wasn't topped, the miner's pay was docked."

The coal operators also hired weighing men who routinely docked each car for a set amount of rubble, the useless rock that was mixed in with the coal. For instance, even though a topped coal car weighed four tons, the miner was paid for only two or three tons. The rest, the company claimed, was rubble. This angered the miners, who believed that the cars couldn't possibly contain that much rubble.

Sanitation facilities varied from mine to mine. According to Carlo Brunori, "One chamber was used as a toilet by the miners. The stench was bad, and you'd see the red eyes of rats in there." Emil Ermert remembered that there were no designated chambers in the mine where he worked. "The mine workers and the mules just went wherever they happened to be."

Dangers in the Mines

Throughout the day as the miners blasted the coal, the explosions released poisonous gases into the air and disturbed the weight of the mountain. At intervals, miners continued to check for dangerous conditions. To test the air quality, they used their carbide lamps, small teapot-shaped lanterns. With their drills, they tested the ceilings.

"Many a time," said Joseph McCormick, "from inhaling impure air, I staggered through my work just like men that were drunk. My butty would have to take his shirt off and fan me while I was drilling a hole, and I would do the same for him."

Samuel Wentovich, a butty, lived through a cave-in. "I was about a mile underground. I could hear the timbers squeezing and breaking as I loaded the car up. . . . All of a sudden, twenty feet from me, *boom!* [The roof] started coming down and pushed the sides in. I got caught under a big rock, and I couldn't get out. My leg was broken. There I was all alone. No light. Complete darkness. Every ten, fifteen minutes the squeezing came again, for five or six hours. I lay there, waiting. Finally, the rescuers got to me and carried me out on a stretcher. When I came out, there were a couple hundred people waiting for me. They all started yelling, cheering."

Sometimes the blasting caused disastrous explosions, especially if dangerous gas had been present. "After an explosion," said Ferdinand Woll, "three gangway men were seriously burned, another was knocked over by the force of the explosion, and in falling, struck the car rail and suffered a permanently crippled arm. One man had his face and head singed bare. Panic-stricken, the man raced

Superstitious mine workers preferred to ride in the same seat in the man-trip cars and to eat in the same spot each day.

Pennsylvania Historical and Museum Commission, Bureau of Historic Sites and Museums, Anthracite Museum Complex

out through the gangway to the slope, jumped on a trip going up, got outside, and never stopped running until he reached his favorite saloon, where he had a whiskey and a beer."

Superstitions

Most mine workers were superstitious. They liked to eat in the same spot every day, eat with the same friends, and ride in the same seat in the man-trip cars to and from the mines.

They believed that certain actions courted disaster. No miner began a new job or moved on a Friday. Once a miner put away his tools and started home, he would never, for any reason, return to his chamber, for that would sorely tempt the fates.

It was also considered bad luck for a woman to enter a mine, because the mine workers believed some women could put a curse on the mine. It was bad enough, they thought, to be working so close to Satan's domain.

Some miners even considered it bad luck to meet a woman on their way to work. If they did, they would curse their luck, go back home, then start out again. For that reason, many women wouldn't leave their homes to pick coal until well after the mine workers were in the mines.

In the mines, unknown sounds were attributed to ghosts. The mine workers believed mules could see ghosts and spirits that were invisible to the human eye. These ghosts and spirits, the workers claimed, belonged to mine workers who had been killed by a roof fall or explosion or other mining accident. After a tragedy, the butties and friends of the deceased mine worker put their tools down and refused to work until after the funeral. They claimed this was the only way to properly drive a ghost out of a mine after an accident.

Despite their superstitious natures, the men and boys enjoyed spinning tall tales about ghosts and playing ghostly tricks on other workers by pretending to be the spirit of someone who had died. Once, two boys smuggled a goat into the mines. They strapped a brightly lit candle between the goat's horns, then turned it loose in the gangway. The eerie bobbing of the candle petrified a group of mine workers.

The creaking, groaning, and hissing sounds of the working mine were often attributed to ghosts.
Wyoming Historical and Geological Society

For many years the mine bosses and owners tried to convince mine workers that their fears were unfounded. They said that the mysterious knocking and moaning sounds were simply the natural workings of the mine. But in a job that was so precarious and subject to the whim of nature, the mine workers were unmoved by any logical explanation. Perhaps, for them, it was better to let fate rest in the hands of the unknown.

5 The Patch Village

Each day, before it was light out, my mother sent my sister and me to the culm banks to pick coal for our coal stove. The neighbors would hear my wagon creaking along the dark streets. We'd fill the wagon with coal, then hurry home, get washed up, and go to school. The next day we'd go pick coal again.

— *Lil Ferretti*

Paul Thomas Studio, Shamokin, Pennsylvania

The coal operators didn't live in their company houses or patch villages. They lived in large mansions in cities like Wilkes-Barre, Scranton, and Philadelphia or on country estates.

Lewis Hine Collection, Albin O. Kuhn Library, University of Maryland, Baltimore County

For the most part, the coal land was owned by powerful businessmen like Stephen Girard, who was known as America's wealthiest man in the 1830s. The coal landowners leased their property to coal operators—enterprising men like John Markle, who built the breakers, erected patch villages, and hired men to mine the coal. In return for the right to mine coal, the operators paid the coal landowners a royalty on all the coal that came out of their land.

The coal landowners and operators shared similar backgrounds and beliefs. They were primarily descendants of old-stock colonial families and graduates of prestigious colleges or colleges that had good engineering programs. They also shared capitalistic dreams of acquiring great

66

wealth, which they accomplished through the labor of the mine workers.

In return for their power and wealth, most owners and operators believed they were obligated to act as trustees for their workers. As John Markle put it, they were responsible for the "proper use of them." For the mine workers, it was insulting to be treated as though they were incapable of taking care of themselves.

Some coal mines were located near free towns like Scranton, Wilkes-Barre, and Pottsville, where more fortunate miners could own their own homes and where more employment opportunities, in such places as factories, existed. But even there, the coal company was a powerful influence.

Other mine workers and their families lived in patch villages, which were hastily constructed and owned by men like John Markle. In the patch village, everything—the colliery, the long rows of company housing, the company store, the church, the school, and the police—was owned by the coal company. The coal operator wanted to accommodate as many miners as possible, because the more miners a coal company had, the more coal it could mine and the more profit it could make.

Company Houses

The patch village was laid out according to the class of worker. At the head of the streets, the mine bosses and supervisors lived in large, comfortable homes. Next came the miners' houses, which usually had two rooms—a large kitchen area downstairs and a garret, or attic, upstairs where the children slept. Thin pieces of wood were nailed over the outside seams but did little to keep out the rain and the cold. On the inside, most walls had no plastering. Few houses had cellars or foundations. Outhouses, usually shared by at least two families, stood in the backyards. Chickens, dogs, cats, pigs, and goats ran free.

Samuel Wentovich remembered what it was like to live in a tiny house: "There were twelve of us kids. There were three of us boys in one bed. The girls slept four to a bed because there were more girls. Instead of lengthwise, we'd sleep crossways. I used to tie my end of the blanket to the end of the bed so nobody could steal it. My brother used to pull it off me."

Butties and other unskilled workers lived in shacks at the bottom of the streets or along the side streets. Sometimes as many as twenty or thirty people crowded into one shack, which was described as teeming with vermin. The people took turns sleeping in shifts.

The patch village was also divided into ethnic sections, as the immigrants clustered together with others from their homelands. In one village, it was possible to visit

The kitchen coal stove heated the miner's house. In winter, bricks were heated in the stove and then used to warm the beds. On cold nights, three or four bricks were used for one bed.
Joseph Bartoletti, Moscow, Pennsylvania

68

Scotch Road, Dago Street, Murphy's Patch, Welsh Hill, and Hun Town. The streets were filled with the sound of different languages and the smell of ethnic foods.

The coal company charged high rent for housing, which was deducted from the worker's pay. To help make ends meet, almost every family took in several boarders from the old country. Some boarders were single, but others were married men who were saving money to send for their wives and families. For a few dollars a month, the boarders got a place to stay, meals prepared, lunches packed, and clothing washed and ironed.

Immigrants from twenty-six different European countries settled in the anthracite region.

Pennsylvania Historical and Museum Commission, Bureau of Historic Sites and Museums, Anthracite Museum Complex

69

Houses built directly over the mines or on culm banks often collapsed when the ground shifted.

Postcard Collection of Charles Kumpas, Clarks Summit, Pennsylvania

Most coal operators didn't care about the safety or condition of the miners' houses. Outhouses were erected too close to water supplies, and open sewage ran through many streets. Some houses squatted on or between the culm banks, the loose piles of refuse from the breaker. Others were built directly over the mines on land that had been weakened considerably from mining. If the culm or the land beneath the house shifted, the house collapsed or caved in. One family had to move when the kitchen caved in, swallowing the furniture. They managed to rescue the coal stove just as it began to slip in. Another family built a bridge to get to the outhouse after their backyard caved in.

Legally, the coal operator could do what he wanted with the houses he owned. One day in 1890 when Edward Monaghan returned from his shift at the mines, he discovered that his house had been torn down because the coal operator had decided he needed more space for a culm bank. Monaghan, his invalid wife, and their seven children found themselves homeless.

Monday, Wash Day

Throughout coal country, mothers and daughters worked side by side. For them, Monday meant wash day; Tuesday, ironing; Wednesday, baking; Thursday, sewing; Friday, cleaning; Saturday, shopping and bathing; and Sunday, church, rest, and recreation.

Women wait their turn at a pump that supplied twenty-five families with water.

Pennsylvania Historical and Museum Commission, Bureau of Historic Sites and Museums, Anthracite Museum Complex

Many patch villages had water pumps that were shared by as many as twenty-five families. To prepare for laundry and bathing, women and children waited in line for their turn at the pump and carried the buckets of water home. As one complained, "It's hard to get at keeping clean when you're tired from carrying all that water."

Most of the cooking was done on the kitchen coal stove, but the stove was often moved outside to a shed during the summer months, when the weather became too hot to cook indoors. Baking was done outdoors year-round in

71

On Mondays, women washed the clothes.
Canal Museum at Hugh Moore Park,
Easton, Pennsylvania

large brick ovens erected in the backyards. Bread was a staple of every miner's lunch, and depending on the size of the family, twenty or more loaves of bread were baked each week.

The company houses turned black and gloomy from the soot that billowed out of the coal breaker. To brighten up their homes, families erected colorful birdhouses outside. Every family planted a garden and raised livestock, and the children helped their mothers tend fruits and vegetables, medicinal herbs and roots, chickens, ducks, rabbits, and pigeons. Some coal companies offered prizes for the best garden or the largest tomato.

Helen Fedorsha, who grew up in Eckley Village, described how she cared for her family's garden: "There were no insecticides. You'd go through the potato patch with a can with some kerosene and water in it. You'd look under the leaves . . . and if there were potato bug eggs under there, you'd nip the leaf off and put it in the kerosene. If you found potato bugs, you'd hold the bucket under the bush and hit the bush. You'd shake the bugs into the kerosene and water. That would kill them."

Each family owned a cow or two. During the day, the cows grazed the open pastures and woods. At night, the children chased the cows home. "In the evening, when the cows came home from grazing, all you could hear was the tinkling of bells," recalled Helen. "Our cow would come in the back alley, and there was a fence and a gate. She'd put her head over the gate and she'd *moooo!* That way, we knew she was home and it was time to feed her up and milk her."

Alex McLaughlin remembered his family's cow: "We had a cow until the day she sank into a mine cave. When we found her, she was twenty-five feet below the surface. It must have been a gradual subsidence because the cow didn't seem hurt. But my father decided to kill her there and carry the meat home because of all the trouble it would take to get her out again."

Throughout coal country, people gathered and prepared food together. The men made smoked sausage and kielbasa in their backyards. They made sauerkraut and wine in large wooden barrels. Neighbors swapped canned foods to enjoy a greater variety over the long winter months. Families picked blueberries to can and sell, and in

Pearl Agostini (later Santarelli), at age twelve, stands behind her mother in this family portrait.

Family photograph, Joseph Bartoletti, Moscow, Pennsylvania

the evenings they plucked feathers from ducks and geese to make pillows and down comforters.

By thirteen, most girls had learned all the skills they needed to take care of a house and raise a family. "I was thirteen when I married," said Pearl Santarelli. "Massimino was twenty. I wanted to go out and play with the other girls, but I couldn't because I was a married woman. I had to stay home and cook and clean for my husband." At fourteen, Pearl had her first baby.

When a mother became sick or died, relatives and neighbors took the motherless children in and raised them, despite having their own large families.

Or the responsibility fell to the oldest daughter. "My mother had nine children and she was thirty-five when she died," said Mary Marshlik. "My oldest sister wasn't quite fourteen and our youngest was a year and a half. My sister took care of us. She did everything by hand. The men's workclothes were spread out on the washboard, and she used a scrub brush to wash them. She wrung them out by hand. Our underpants were made from flour bags and she put lace on them."

The Company Store

Each patch village had a store that was owned by the coal company. Women bought flour, sugar, and other foodstuff that they couldn't grow or make. Men bought powder, squibs, oil, and other mining supplies. On payday, children

who had a nickel to spend bought candy and ice cream.

The company store was a good source of profit for the coal company, especially when shopkeepers forced the miners and their families to pay exorbitant prices for inferior-quality goods. If the miners complained or made purchases elsewhere, they feared losing their jobs or being evicted from their houses. One shopkeeper admitted that he inflated the prices as much as 200 percent—oil valued at twenty-five cents was sold for seventy-five cents, and a ninety-cent keg of blasting powder for three dollars. It was no small wonder that the mine workers called the company store the "pluck-me" store.

At the company store, customers could buy "off the book" or on credit. The storekeeper kept track of the purchases, and payment was deducted from the workers' wages. On payday, it wasn't unusual for a mine worker to find out that his pay equaled his deductions or—even

The company police spied on the workers and their families, reporting what they saw to the coal operators. The police also served as collection officers and pressured workers to pay their debts.

Canal Museum at Hugh Moore Park, Easton, Pennsylvania

worse—that he was in debt to the company store.

Alex McLaughlin remembered the payday he earned twenty-eight dollars but had only forty-five cents after deductions. Later, nearly four dollars was deducted for underwear he never bought. When he complained, he was told, "You better keep quiet if you want to keep your job."

Not all company stores were corrupt. When a family fell on hard times because of illness or other tragedy, some shopkeepers extended credit or charity. Sophia Coxe, wife of coal operator Eckley Coxe, was known as the "Angel of the Anthracite" throughout part of the anthracite region. She took care of the widows and the orphans and others who were suffering through hard times. She paid their bills and took care of other necessities.

In free coal towns, the stores were privately owned, but even there, the coal company often used its influence to urge miners to patronize certain businesses. The mine workers still appreciated the honest shopkeeper. "My mother had her own big book at her store," said Gabriella Slivinski, daughter of an Old Forge shopkeeper. "She kept a record of what everybody bought. She knew when the paydays were, and some people paid in full and others asked to be carried. My mother took people at their word. But a lot of people would stick her."

The Culm Banks

Although the mine workers and their families could usually buy their coal at reduced prices from the coal company, many were too stubborn to pay for the coal they dug from the earth. Others were too poor. Each day, women and children could be seen searching the culm banks for the chunks of good coal that were thrown out with the rubble.

Technically, picking coal was stealing, since the refuse was company property. The culm banks were guarded by the company police, who patrolled all of the colliery's property, looking for people who were breaking the coal operator's law. Some police looked the other way, but others smashed the pickers' baskets, wagons, and wheelbarrows. Some even searched the mine workers' homes for evidence of picked coal. If found out, the families had to pay fines and pay for the coal. Often, they were charged for more than they actually picked.

Picking coal at the culm banks was dangerous because the loose ground could shift and bury the pickers.
Wyoming Historical and Geological Society

These women and children are on their way home from scavenging coal at the culm banks.
Wyoming Historical and Geological Society

The police, however, weren't the only danger. Sometimes the loose culm collapsed beneath the pickers' feet, burying the the pickers and suffocating them. Gabriella Slivinski remembered a neighbor woman who died that way: "One day, we were waiting for her to come

home, and she never did. We found out she went too high up [on the culm bank], and there was a cave-in and it swallowed her."

School

Many children attended school, but often for a few years at most. Just like students in other parts of the country, they pledged allegiance to the flag, listened to readings from the Bible, and studied lessons in reading, writing, arithmetic, geography, and history.

For immigrant children, this also meant learning how to speak, read, and write in English. Without special classes or language teachers to help, older children were placed in classes with much younger children. "I should have been in the fourth grade," said Massimino Santarelli, "but I didn't know any English. So they sent me to first. I was the biggest child there. My knees wouldn't fit beneath the desk."

Some schools were free; in others, the students paid tuition, bought their own books, and if the classes were held at night, they had to supply the oil for their lamps. "When I was in fifth grade," said Samuel Wentovich, "they had a library. Anybody who wanted to use the library had to pay two cents each week. Two cents to me was like a million dollars. The teacher came to me and said, 'Can't you get two cents for the library?' I said I couldn't because my father drank and we never got anything. The next day she told me, 'You can go to the library without paying.' She never told anybody that I didn't pay."

Discipline was strict. The wooden paddle was used to dole out punishment to students who broke the rules or didn't learn their lessons. Some paddles had holes drilled into them, which created a painful suction effect upon contact. "You only got hit twice," said Joe Charnigo, "but with the suction of the paddle, you wouldn't sit down for a while."

Many children attended one-room schoolhouses that were heated by coal stoves. The children often picked and sold blueberries to buy school clothes and shoes.

Paul Thomas Studio, Shamokin, Pennsylvania

Children walked to school with friends.

And as Leo Slivinski recalled, "You wouldn't go home and tell your parents, because if you did, you'd get it again."

The children soon found they had difficulty concentrating on school when they knew how badly their parents needed money to pay for rent, food, medical bills, and other necessities. By the time they were ten years old, most children quit school to help their families.

Not all children felt the obligation to work. Some ran away. "I told my father I did not intend to spend the rest of my life working in the coal mines," said Alex McLaughlin. He and a friend hopped a train, but Alex soon returned home—and to the Sandy Banks mines—after his friend was killed jumping from the train.

Others looked forward to being free of school. "It was a disgrace to go to school," said William O'Boyle, who followed his older brother to work at the mines. "Only sissies

80

went to school. All the regular fellows got jobs in the breaker picking slate or in the mines nippin' [tending door]. Even the parents took this attitude toward schooling. The boy who worked was their favorite."

Still others had a strong sense of duty and responsibility. Richard Owens enjoyed school, but when his foster father died from miner's lung, he knew his foster mother needed his wages. "There was a need for somebody to go to work," said Richard, who quit school in the sixth grade. "And so I did."

6 After a Hard Day's Work

Many a time I cried with the pain [from picking slate], but yet when the whistle blew for quitting time in the evening, I was as happy as a king to know I had finished another day and added another quarter to my pay to help support my family.

— Joseph McCormick

Scranton Times, Scranton, Pennsylvania

Quitting Time

Fathers and sons knew no work other than mining. After years of mining, the workers' flesh became ingrained with blue-black specks of coal.
Wyoming Historical and Geological Society

When full coal was reached, the shift ended. The mine workers headed back to the cage or man-trip cars, which carried them out of the mines. In the breaker, the machinery stopped, the coal stopped flowing, and the sooty-faced breaker boys left their pine seats. The men and boys walked home, their skin black from coal dust and their wet clothing heavy with dirt.

At home, mothers had hot bath water waiting on the stove. They poured the water into a big wooden or galvanized metal tub. The tub was too small to fit in comfortably, so the men and boys knelt and leaned over its sides in order to wash themselves a little bit at a time. "Sometimes," remembered Web Snyder, "there would be as many as three around the tub at the same time."

The women helped the men—including the boarders. "We would wash their backs," explained Helen Fedorsha, who grew up in Eckley Village. "They would wash all the rest themselves. There weren't bought washcloths at that time. We used underwear that was worn out."

Dirty workclothes were hung behind the coal stove to dry for the next day. "When my father came home," said Mary Fanucci, "his trousers were so heavy with water and dirt because he worked on his knees. He would wear the clothes for one week and then we would wash them."

Each night the mine workers bathed in wooden or galvanized metal tubs. The rest of the family bathed on Saturday nights.

National Archives

Recreation

After work, if the workers weren't too tired, they made time for recreation. Some mine patches were "dry," which meant that no alcohol was sold, but in most patches as well as free towns, pubs and saloons were common. Every third or fourth house was a pub, claimed outsiders, and pub signs hung in as many as six different languages.

At the pubs, the men filled their lunch pails with beer to take home (called "growlers") or stopped in for a shot of whiskey and a beer, which they believed was good for

On Sunday afternoons, entire patch villages turned out for the company-sponsored ball games.

Wyoming Historical and Geological Society

clearing the coal dust from their lungs. The men spent hours in the pub, singing ballads, playing cards, telling stories, reciting poems, and dancing jigs. Prizes were awarded for the best entertainment.

Other sorts of competitions were common, too. "Most of the mine workers were powerful men," remembered Stephen O'Boyle. "They boasted as to who could do the most work or perform the strongest physical feat. Contests of many kinds were common—foot-racing, weight lifting—and I have seen miners endeavoring to see which pair could drill a hole in a rock in the fastest time, even after a day's work."

Coal companies organized football and baseball teams, and soon every patch had its own team. Amid the coal dust and the culm banks, the teams competed against other mine patches, and the Sunday games became the highlight of the week. Entire villages turned out to cheer, even though it often meant packing lunches and walking several miles one way. Often, other coal companies tried to steal good players by offering them better jobs.

The boys formed their own teams, too, and practiced in the streets after work until it was dark. Equipment such as balls and gloves was expensive and hard to come by, so the boys played with homemade baseballs that were constructed of string wrapped around a rubber ball and covered with black electrical tape. Or the boys captured foul balls from the men's games. Often, only the first baseman and catcher had gloves; the other boys used bare hands or old leather work gloves from the mine.

Joe Boley, who later became a major-league baseball player with the Philadelphia Athletics, remembered his first baseball glove: "I pleaded with my mother and father to buy me a baseball glove. At first they thought it was a waste of money, but finally they agreed to buy it. My love for baseball was so great, there were times I just threw the ball against a barn door or concrete wall and ran over and fielded it."

Children rode homemade sleds in the winter.
Canal Museum at Hugh Moore Park, Easton, Pennsylvania

In wintertime the children carried homemade sleds to the huge snow-covered culm banks and held sleigh-riding parties. Some fashioned skis from the wooden staves of sauerkraut barrels. When they got home, they dried their shoes in the oven. Mary Fanucci remembered the time she forgot about her shoes drying in the oven. "The next morning they were all roasted and they were the only pair I had. My father got me a pair of high-cuts—the kind the boys wore. I felt so ashamed when I had to go to school because I had to wear boys' shoes."

In the summer, the children swam in the black water

that collected in the strippings—the deep holes left by strip mining—or in the brackish ponds that formed from the breaker runoff. "My mother always knew when I was swimming," said Leo Slivinski, "because I'd come home black from head to toe."

When the circus came to town, it meant more problems for the colliery operators and the breaker boss. All of the boys wanted to see the circus, but the colliery operators wanted the boys to work. "Once, when the bosses insisted on us working," said Jack Stanton, "some of the boys sneaked in [the breaker] at six-thirty in the morning on circus day and cut the main belt. When the boss tried to start the machinery up, it would not turn. There was nothing for us to do but go home for the day." The boys, of course, went to the circus.

Eventually, movies came to the free towns in coal country. On Saturdays, the children paid a nickel for a movie ticket and gathered in the balconies. Joe Mickatavage described a typical afternoon at the movies: "Up in the balcony, the guys would be chewing tobacco and they'd spit on the floor. You could float on the tobacco juice. Oh, what a mess! Then when the movie started, they'd be screaming and hollering, and—oh, boy—it's a wonder the balcony didn't crash down. It was a crazy place."

Payday

Payday came once or twice a month, depending on the colliery. On payday, mine workers of all ages gathered

On payday, mine workers and their families dressed in their best clothing to collect their pay.

Pennsylvania Historical and Museum Commission, Bureau of Historic Sites and Museums, Anthracite Museum Complex

early at the company office and waited patiently for the company police to throw open the window. It was common for women to collect their husband's pay, before the men had a chance to drink it away at the pubs.

Soon the paymaster took his seat at the window and opened the company strongbox. As each mine worker approached the paymaster's window, he handed the paymaster a due bill or pay voucher. The paymaster then counted out the right number of gold and silver pieces and dropped them into a small envelope and handed it to the worker. Paper currency—folding money—wasn't trusted by many people, especially immigrants, and it wasn't widely used until later years.

Nearly every boy turned his pay over to his mother, and in return, he was given a few nickels or a quarter to spend. The younger boys flocked to the store to buy candy, ice cream, and soda; the older boys were more interested in the

89

In the early 1900s, there were 366 breakers in anthracite coal country, employing over 140,000 workers. Some breakers employed as many as one hundred boys.

Paul Thomas Studio, Shamokin, Pennsylvania

slot machines, cock fights, saloons, and dances. Even after they reached adulthood and were married, most mine workers continued to hand at least part of their pay over to their mothers.

Often the boys participated in a "knockdown." From their pay, they withheld a few nickels before giving it to their mother. Because they knew that mothers have a habit of comparing notes, the boys decided beforehand on the set amount of the knockdown.

Eager to save what little money they could, many families hid their money in trunks or sewed it in garments. Pearl Santarelli remembered hiding the bonds her husband brought home. "They weren't much, but they were all the savings we had. I locked it in an old trunk, and I hid the trunk inside an old coal stove in our cellar. I only used that old coal stove a few times a year when it was time to can the vegetables. Canning time came around. I lit the coal stove, and soon I smelled something burning. And then I remembered. I screamed and I took out the trunk. The trunk was all burned, but luckily the bonds were all right."

Anna Cardoni's uncle hid his money behind the jars of

90

canned food. "One day he came yelling to my mother that someone had stolen his money," said Anna. "He pointed to where it had been hidden. My mother looked but all she saw was a pile of paper that looked like a bunch of cotton. Mice had chewed all his money."

Old-World Ways

Most of the immigrants who settled in coal country were from small farming villages in Europe. "There was no work in Italy," remembered Massimino Santarelli. "My uncles were already in the United States, working in the mines. They wrote and told us that much work could be found in the mines."

Eager for work, Massimino and his family crossed the Atlantic Ocean by steamship in the early 1900s, arriving at Ellis Island in New York. From there, a train carried them over a hundred more miles to Jessup, Pennsylvania. "My uncles found us a place to stay and work," Massimino recalled.

Small numbers of African-Americans, Canadians, Mexicans, Puerto Ricans, and South Americans also worked in the mines. Here, they transplanted their customs, religion, language, and other ethnic ways.

Children and their families enjoyed the same ethnic foods they ate in the old country. Those from the northwest countries of Europe such as England, Scotland, Wales, and Ireland ate beef stews, potatoes, and puddings. People from eastern European countries such as Lithuania,

Romania, and Poland enjoyed pork, kielbasa, soups, and breads. Southern Europeans such as Greeks, Italians, and Sicilians preferred spaghetti, tomato sauces, salads, and spicy meats like salami and sausage.

All immigrants celebrated holy days and life events such as births, weddings, and funerals just as they had in their old countries. Christians celebrated Christmas and Easter; Jews observed Hanukkah and Passover. Parents played matchmaker for unmarried daughters. Italian honeymooners were serenaded at two or three o'clock in the morning by singers who wouldn't leave until they were invited in and given something to eat. And Slavic families and their friends prepared feasts to welcome new babies.

Funerals in coal country were often held in the living room. The body was packed in ice and placed in a coffin. The coffin lay on a table or across two chairs. During the three-day wake, the coffin was left open so that the dead person could be presented for the last time. Women gathered around the dead body, never leaving it unattended throughout the wake. The men gathered in the kitchen, where they smoked and ate and told ghost stories. Many families took photographs with the deceased. For Irish families, it was customary to pay funeral criers to weep and wail over the deceased—whether they knew the dead person or not.

The immigrants' ethnic values remained the same. Throughout coal country, people approached life in much the same way as they had in the old country, where life and

Families often posed for photographs with the deceased.

Donald L. Miller and Richard E. Sharpless,
The Kingdom of Coal.

work rhythms centered around family ties and the village. Babies were born at home, and the women gathered to help the mother. "Whenever my mother was expecting another baby," said Samuel Wentovich, "the neighbors would be there as soon as their husbands left for work at six o'clock in the morning. They would help her all day. When it was time, my sisters would run for the midwife. We all celebrated whenever a baby was born."

Families depended upon each other for support and assistance. They found jobs for relatives and paid for their passage from the old country. Extended families shared housing and tended each other in times of injury or sickness.

7 The Black Maria

My dad ate his lunch in the same spot every day. One day another miner was in his spot, and so he sat on the other side. Suddenly, the roof caved in on him. His back was broken, and he never walked again. When he came home from the hospital, he told me, "You aren't ever to go into a mine. I have worked in the mines enough for all of us." And I never have. I never will.

— John Sutkowsky

When the breaker whistle cried at an odd hour, it meant only one thing to the families: disaster at the mines. Women and children ran down the streets to the colliery, where they implored the other workers, the foremen, anyone, to tell them who was hurt or killed.

Coal country was a tragic place to live and work because of the geology of the mines. Anthracite coal lay in steep veins that pitched high inside mountains or reached deep into the earth, often below the water table. The richest vein, for instance, lay precariously close to the bed of the Susquehanna River. These factors made anthracite extremely dangerous to mine.

The Worst Offense

It has been estimated that at least one anthracite worker was killed daily in Pennsylvania coal country. Nearly every family experienced tragedy, leaving widows, fatherless children, and grief-stricken parents.

The coal company wanted coal from their mines, not injured workers and broken bodies. Stopping work to help the injured or take care of the dead meant the colliery would lose money. "The worst offense a worker could commit against the coal company was to be injured," said one miner. "Without fail, if a worker was injured, the mine boss would heap upon him the rottenest and dirtiest language he could think of."

In one instance, when work stopped in one area, the colliery superintendent noticed that a man was dead. "Just lay him on the side," he told the workers, "until you finish dumping this coal."

The most frequent accidents occurred when large pieces of loose rock crashed down on the workers, flattening them and grinding them so severely into the floor that

Caught Under Fall of Roof
in Anthracite Coal Mine.

*The majority of accidents resulted
from roof falls.*
Wyoming Historical and Geological Society

their bodies had to be scraped up with shovels. Workers who survived the rock falls were left horribly mangled. Some were paralyzed from crushed spines or had splintered limbs that could never be set properly.

Joseph McCormick remembered when a young boy who was hired to drive the mule met with tragedy. "The boy worked two days and seemed to be getting along nicely, but at quitting time on the second day, when he should have passed through my door, there was no sign of him. The loader boss told me to go help him out. I found his

98

mule all twisted up in his traces and spreader chains and no sign of the driver. Then I saw the driver's head sticking out from under the wagon. He was dead. It took three men to lift the wagon off him."

Until the turn of the century, the collieries didn't have stretchers, first aid, or ambulances. Most workers did not know much about emergency care. "Little could be done to relieve suffering or to save a life," claimed Rudy Schneider. "If a worker lost a leg, arm, or other body part, or if he suffered a puncture wound or deep cut, all they knew to do was lift him up on a mine plank and take him outside. There he was loaded by a company team, powered with a couple of stubborn mules, and taken to his home."

The collieries took little or no responsibility for the injuries and deaths of their workers, so it was up to the workers to do what they could. To each disaster, the workers and the community responded, risking their own lives to rescue their friends, and if rescue failed, to recover their friends' bodies. Mine workers knew they could count on each other.

"If a man was injured or killed," said Carlo Brunori, "no matter how dangerous it was, they'd go in there to get him out. It was the code of the mines." For many, such a code meant working under extremely dangerous conditions. Rescuers never knew when a weak roof would begin squeezing again or if there would be another explosion.

It also meant working without pay: the colliery only paid for coal that was removed from the mines, not bodies.

This young boy lost both his legs in a mining accident. There was a time when a miner wasn't considered injured unless he had lost an arm, an eye, or a leg.

Lewis Hine Collection, Albin O. Kuhn Library, University of Maryland, Baltimore County

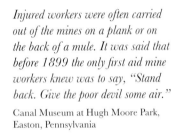

Injured workers were often carried out of the mines on a plank or on the back of a mule. It was said that before 1899 the only first aid mine workers knew was to say, "Stand back. Give the poor devil some air."

Canal Museum at Hugh Moore Park, Easton, Pennsylvania

But for those workers determined to rescue a friend or search for bodies, the danger and financial loss weren't the worst part. "That was bad work, going in there, picking up pieces," remembered one rescuer. "An arm here, a leg there, here a fellow with his belly blowed open, a man with no head, his brains splashed against the rib, dead pit mules all blowed to pieces. . . . Couldn't eat after that."

The Black Maria

Eventually, the collieries provided horse-drawn ambulances called Black Marias to carry bodies home. As the black carriage rattled its way down the street, it attracted everyone's attention. Women and children ran up to the driver, asking who the victim was.

100

The ambulance driver couldn't answer. He had to comply with the "next-of-kin" rule, meaning he had to notify the closest relative of the deceased first.

Mary Fanucci remembered the day the Black Maria came down her street. "When I was seven, the breaker whistle blew. I knew immediately that it meant somebody had been killed in the mines. A little while later, men carried a body on a long wicker basket to my neighbor's house. The body was our neighbor, and the men who carried him were his fellow workers. The body lay on the wicker basket, all dirty, just the way it was in the mines. The men took the body to the wife's kitchen and left it there. The wife had to wash the body and get it ready to be buried. For a long time, a black ribbon hung on the door."

The old man with the crutch was injured in the mines. When miners became too old or were unable to work underground, they often returned to the breakers. "Once a miner, twice a breaker boy" was a popular saying.

George Bretz Collection, Albin O. Kuhn Library, University of Maryland, Baltimore County

Foreign workers who lived in boarding houses posed a problem because their families still lived in the old country. If other immigrants claimed the body, it meant they would have to bear the funeral expense, which they often couldn't afford. As a result, the unclaimed bodies of boarders were given to a medical school, where they were used in anatomy classes.

The loss of a father had dire consequences on families. Without insurance, widows and children faced eviction from the company housing because they couldn't pay the rent. In order to protect their families, the mine workers made monthly contributions to a "keg fund." In the event of a tragedy, the fund was usually just enough to help a family cover funeral expenses and the rent for a short period of time. The deceased miner's tools were also raffled off, and the proceeds were given to the family. After that, the families were on their own.

More generous collieries set aside housing called "Widows' Row." In return for the housing, the widows had to agree to take in boarders. This, in turn, provided more workers for the colliery and enabled the colliery to make even more money.

Major Tragedies

Some of the worst mining disasters occurred in the deep mines of anthracite coal country. Workers could expect to suffer several serious injuries and to experience all sorts of accidents during their years of employment.

Some accidents could not have been avoided; mining was a dangerous job that left people subject to the whim of nature. Other accidents resulted from a lack of supervision or from carelessness—loose rock that should have been removed, more timbers that should have been installed, improper blasting techniques, or failure to follow company regulations. This was the case in Wilkes-Barre's Baltimore Tunnel explosion in 1919, when seven men carried kegs of black powder on the man-trip cars, even though company regulations forbade it. The man-trip cars had descended two hundred feet when the dynamite exploded, roasting men alive, blowing others to bits, and suffocating still more. In all, the explosion killed ninety-two people.

Sometimes no laws existed to protect the workers. In 1869, coal mines were not required to have two openings. As a result, when the Avondale mine shaft caught on fire, there was no way for the one hundred and ten men and boys to escape, and many burned to death. According to a reporter, the saddest sight of all was the bodies of fathers and sons who died in each other's arms.

And then there were times when the colliery continued to operate in spite of dangerous conditions. In 1896, the miners at the Pittston Twin Shaft Colliery knew the roof was unstable and notified the mine officials. Rather than stop work, the company ordered additional men to put in extra props over the weekend so that the miners could still work on Monday.

However, in the middle of Saturday night, over one hundred acres of rock and coal collapsed. The fifty-eight men who were installing the timbers were buried alive. Rescue operations began immediately but were halted as the roof continued to fall in and the Susquehanna River rose slowly in the gangway. As days passed, all hope of saving the miners disappeared, and their bodies were never recovered.

Ten-year-old Willie Hatton and his father were among the fathers and sons who died during the Avondale disaster.
Joseph Bartoletti, Moscow, Pennsylvania

8 Strike!

As I saw those eager eyes peering at me from eager little faces, the fight had new meaning for me; I felt that I was fighting for the boys, fighting a battle for innocent childhood.

— John Mitchell, labor organizer

In St. Gabriel's Cemetery in Hazleton, Pennsylvania, John Brislen's epitaph reads: "Fourty [sic] years I worked with pick & drill / Down in the mines against my will, / The Coal Kings slave, but now it's passed; / Thanks be to God I am free at last."

Joseph Bartoletti, Moscow, Pennsylvania

T he old-world ways of many immigrants seemed strange and frightening to the Americans who had lived and worked in coal country all of their lives. To make matters worse, the coal operators preferred to hire the immigrants who were so hard-working, willing to do more dangerous work, and willing to put up with deplorable conditions. Some Americans feared that the immigrants would take jobs away from them. In 1870, for instance, three Scranton coal companies fired their experienced miners and replaced them with German and Irish immigrants.

As a result, the immigrants met with prejudice and discrimination. Newcomers were often pelted with stones and sticks as they got off the trains. The mine bosses gave some nationalities better jobs than others and illegally taxed some immigrants. Even the train conductors and brakemen played mean tricks by hustling the immigrants onto train and trolley cars and putting them off at the wrong stations. Men wearing fake government buttons often extorted money from the immigrants.

Because of the terrible conditions and unfair practices the mine workers faced, they tried to form unions and strike. The immigrants, often the poorest class, played a major role in union activities.

The coal miners wanted shorter work days, more money, better living conditions, an end to compulsory purchases at the company store, and an end to discrimination. The first recorded strike occurred in 1842, but it failed to unite the mine workers. From 1865 until 1897, several other small strikes occurred, but these attempts also foundered because it was difficult organizing people who spoke so many different languages and who didn't trust each other. After each strike, it seemed that conditions for the mine workers only worsened. But the men, women, and children of coal country continued to grow desperate for reform.

Some fought back by forming secret societies. The most famous society was the secret Irish group known as the Molly Maguires. From 1864 until about 1875, the Mollies wreaked havoc and terror throughout coal country. To get

The secret organization of the Molly Maguires sent coffin notices to bosses they didn't like.

Historical Society of Schuylkill County, Pottsville, Pennsylvania

even with the coal companies, they burned company bridges and derailed coal cars. They sent anonymous "coffin notices" to mine bosses that they didn't like. The coffin notices were written threats that promised damage to the bosses' properties, personal injury, or even death if certain grievances weren't put right. If the bosses ignored the threats, the Mollies followed through on their promises.

Franklin B. Gowen, president of Reading Railroad, which owned an interest in many collieries, wanted to crush the mine workers' secret societies and any unionizing attempts. He hired detectives to infiltrate the Molly Maguires, gather information about them, and stir up trouble. His detectives were successful. Eventually, the group's leaders were found out and executed.

Just when it seemed as though things could not get

worse for the people of coal country, the Lattimer Massacre occurred. On September 10, 1897, a group of four hundred striking mine workers marched to Lattimer Patch, a small patch village near the Hazleton Mines. The workers were unarmed and carried only the American flag. However, eighty-seven deputies and a sheriff were dispatched to Lattimer, where they waited with loaded rifles. When the mine workers came into sight, the deputies opened fire. Sixty marchers were shot. Eight died instantly and eleven died later from their wounds.

The Greatest Honor

After the 1897 massacre, the mine workers were convinced more than ever that solidarity would be their most powerful weapon—the entire anthracite region had to strike together.

John Mitchell was a young labor organizer who was moved by the plight of the anthracite mine workers. Born in 1870, he was the son of an Illinois bituminous miner who had been killed in a mining accident when John was six. At twelve, John began to work in the mines; by the time he was eighteen, he had experienced enough to know that the mine workers needed a union. He joined the ranks of the United Mine Workers union and proved to be a tireless and effective organizer. By 1898, his labor efforts in the bituminous mines of Illinois, Indiana, Ohio, and western Pennsylvania had met with success, and he turned his interest to the anthracite region.

In 1900, Mitchell became the anthracite mine workers' leader, and the anthracite miners joined the United Mine Workers. As Mitchell told the new members of the union: "The coal you dig is not Slavic coal or Polish coal or Irish coal. It is coal." At last the union members understood that in spite of their ethnic differences they shared common work and living experiences. In essence, a whole new culture had emerged—a coal culture.

The greatest honor of all was to be a "union man" or "Johnny Mitchell man," and the ranks of new members grew steadily. The boys joined the United Mine Workers, and like their fathers, they held weekly meetings and paid dues. Only members who knew the password were admitted to the meetings.

To have a strong union, the United Mine Workers needed the support of every worker. The boys pressured the non-union miners to join. Mule drivers were especially effective: they refused to deliver empty coal cars to non-union workers. The boys stuck together. If they thought one of their junior members was fired or treated unfairly, they went on strike, bringing the entire mining operation to a halt.

Loyalty spread to the backyards, alleys, churches, and schools. At home, children refused to play with other children whose fathers didn't belong to the union. One small boy, who had been rejected by the other children because his father didn't join the union, pleaded, "I'll be a Johnny Mitchell man, only let me play."

Finally, after a year of organizing, the people of anthracite coal country felt powerful enough to force the coal companies to listen to them. John Mitchell called their first strike on September 17, 1900. The timing was crucial: soon Americans would need anthracite to heat their homes during the long winter months ahead. Surely, the strikers thought, this would force the coal companies to listen to their grievances. Within a week, 125,000 men and boys were striking. Large groups of workers marched from colliery to colliery in order to shut them down, and by early October, nearly every colliery in the anthracite fields was idle.

One troublesome agitator was Mary Harris Jones, the widow of a foundry worker and long-time labor militant. Known as Mother Jones, she also marched from colliery to colliery, convincing men, women, and children to follow her. When the company police threatened to use force to stop her, John Mitchell intervened and asked Mother Jones to curtail her activities.

Public sympathy favored the mine workers as their deplorable living and working conditions made newspaper headlines across the nation, and the coal companies were

Dressed in black and wielding an umbrella, Mother Jones helped organize mine workers by marching from colliery to colliery.
Historical Society of Schuylkill County, Pottsville, Pennsylvania

A young boy scavenges coal from the culm bank and sells each bag for ten cents.

pressured into meeting with the union leaders and discussing their demands.

Finally, the forty-three-day strike of 1900 ended on October 29. Although all of the demands weren't met, the mine workers did win wage increases, and John Mitchell became the mine workers' hero. They voted to make October 29 "Mitchell Day," and when he visited coal country, 20,000 breaker boys paraded before him and presented him with a gold medallion.

John Mitchell continued his fight. The United Mine Workers, bolstered by their first success, spent another year organizing another strike. Although their grievances were the same—they wanted a wage increase, different weighing procedures for the coal, an eight-hour day, and an end to job favoritism—the strike of 1902 would be different. This time, 140,000 mine workers knew they had to stay firm for as long as it took to win their grievances, no matter what the consequences. It was the only way. During the long strike of 1902, coal country united in community spirit. People waved flags, sang ballads to lift morale, hung banners, and marched in parades.

A strike meant the children had plenty of time to attend school, and the children carried their union loyalty to class. The children staged school strikes when they discovered that their teacher or fellow students had family members who were non-union or company bosses or "scab" labor, as workers who crossed the picket lines were called.

112

One school strike was organized during recess by a breaker boy who had discovered his teacher was not a union sympathizer. "We must all hang together now if we wish to assert our manhood," he told the other students. That afternoon, when the teacher's back was turned, the students walked out, sending teachers, the principal, and the community into an uproar. One newspaper account reported a ten-year-old breaker boy, his mouth filled with a wad of tobacco, lamenting, "This school will never amount to nothing until it's organized."

State troops were sent in during strikes to maintain law and order.
Wyoming Historical and Geological Society

Loyalty also spread to the churches. In some parishes, entire classes and choirs disappeared when their teachers and choirmasters weren't union sympathizers. "We won't have a scab teach us," they said.

Women were among those in the front ranks, and they rallied their husbands, sons, and brothers—even threatening them—not to return to work. One woman kept her husband's clothes in the washtub so he wouldn't weaken and cross the picket line. "We might as well starve striking as working," said another woman.

Although the 1902 strike brought great changes to coal country, it also brought much hardship. The strike frightened and angered many people—especially the coal operators who wanted to continue to make huge profits and those who didn't want to pay higher prices for coal. Fearing violence, the coal companies hired additional police and even brought in state troops to protect the collieries' property.

Mother Jones again appeared in the region. She made speeches, calling the coal operators "sewer rats," and organized more labor marches. Big Mary, an immigrant woman, led other women armed with clubs and pieces of scrap iron in charges on the troops.

Some coal operators evicted the mine workers and their families from their company-owned housing. Many mine workers were hungry, penniless, homeless, and scared. Thirty thousand workers fled to other parts of the country hoping to find other work, and fifteen thousand others went back to their homelands. In many families, the oldest children ran away, knowing that extra mouths to feed were a burden. Hundreds of these boys and girls hopped freight trains, called "Johnny Mitchell excursions," and headed for New York and Philadelphia.

As in the Civil War, some families became divided forever when one brother went on strike and the other crossed the picket line to return to work. To the strikers, the most grievous crime of all was to be a scab. Whereas the strike of 1900 was relatively free of violence, the strike of 1902 was not. Feeling betrayed by the scabs, the strikers beat them, stoned them, harassed their families, and even blew up their front porches with dynamite.

To protect the scabs, soldiers escorted them to and from work. However, as one striking miner recalled, "Little did the scabs realize that the soldiers themselves thought less of them [the scabs] than the striking miners did. I remember the soldiers loading up the arms of the small boys in the

Striking mine workers chase a scab through the streets.
Scranton Public Library, Scranton, Pennsylvania

Mine workers and their families were evicted during the 1902 strike.

valley with all sorts of food to take home to their families, who had long since exhausted their food supply and finances."

Finally, President Theodore Roosevelt intervened and appointed an Anthracite Commission to study the miners' grievances. The 1902 strike had lasted 165 days. The outraged public, who feared a severe coal famine was imminent, blamed the coal companies. They said that the operators had violated the public trust by allowing the strike to go on too long and by failing to satisfy the public's need for coal.

Clarence Darrow, the attorney who represented the mine workers at the arbitration hearings, perhaps summed up the struggle best: "They [the coal companies] are fighting for slavery, while we are fighting for freedom. They are fighting for the rule of man over man, for despotism, for darkness, for the past. We are striving to build up man. We are

working for democracy, for humanity, for the future. . . ."

After months of testimony, the Anthracite Commission awarded the mine workers a pay increase, an eight-hour day for certain types of mine work, and weighing men to be paid by the miners, in the hope that this would eliminate unfair dockages. As John Mitchell and others had long hoped, the commission also criticized the employment of children under fourteen.

The inset pictures show John Mitchell (left) and President Theodore Roosevelt (right) above a photograph of the 1902 strike.

Historical Society of Schuylkill County, Pottsville, Pennsylvania

Conclusion

The Legacy of Coal Country

I cried many times. I'm still crying. I had a very hard life.

— *Samuel Wentovich*

Lewis Hine Collection, Library of Congress

After the 1902 strike, labor peace came to the coal fields once again as the mine workers returned to work. For fifteen more years, the anthracite industry continued to grow and reap huge profits. The workers still didn't share in all the profit that resulted from their labor, but they had made progress. The coal operator no longer controlled as much of the mine workers' living conditions. Although company police were still used, the company store was gone. As a result of wage increases and improved working conditions, the mine workers were able to enjoy a higher standard of living. Many even bought their own homes. The improved working and living conditions, in turn, eased ethnic conflict and discrimination.

But what happened to the children of coal country?

It would be nice to say that they fought a battle and won back their childhood. But it didn't happen that way. Despite laws and the fact that child labor had been officially criticized by the Anthracite Commission, children continued to work in the coal mines as long as their parents needed their wages and the coal companies needed their labor. In 1908 the National Child Labor Committee estimated that one out of every four mine workers was a boy, aged seven to sixteen.

Massimino Santarelli worked in the mines for forty-five years, until black lung forced him into retirement. His wife Pearl never learned to read, write, or do arithmetic. They were married sixty-seven years.

Joe Mickatavage became an independent coal operator

during the 1920s. He and his three sons worked their own small "doghole," a coal seam that wasn't profitable enough for a larger company to mine. His son Victor eventually became a federal mine inspector.

Other boys, like Richard Owens, left the mines. After Richard's foster mother remarried, he decided her new husband could take care of her. At twenty-one, he chose to go back to school. "I wanted an education to go into the ministry," said Richard. "I knew I wanted to be a minister since I was eight years old." He returned to high school, then went on to college and became ordained as a Primitive Methodist minister. "By the time I was done," he said, "I had three degrees and I was a minister." Richard Owens served as a pastor until he was ninety-one years old.

Over time, the coal companies found labor that was even cheaper than children: the machine. Eventually, the breaker boys were replaced by mechanized breaking and sorting equipment, the nippers with automated doors, and the spraggers and mule drivers with electric trolleys.

In 1917, anthracite production peaked at one hundred million tons a year, but after World War I, the need for anthracite declined as people turned to oil, gas, coke, and electricity to warm their homes and fuel their transportation and industries. By the end of the 1930s, anthracite was no longer a major industry.

Once the big profits were gone, the coal companies closed their doors and abandoned coal country, leaving thousands of mine workers unemployed. They also left behind barren mountains, abandoned mines, polluted streams and ponds, strippings, mine fires, culm banks, and illnesses such as black lung.

Through the labor of immigrants and children, the United States had broken its dependency on foreign fuel markets and ignited an industrial revolution that made our nation a world power. Anthracite kept millions of people warm and brought together diverse cultures to work for a common goal. But the cost, both human and environmental, was enormous.

Despite their hardships, the mine workers and their families remember the coal days with pride.

"I learned a lot from being together with so many people for so long," said Mary Fanucci. "You don't drift away from that learning."

"I profited from my coal days," said Richard Owens. "I learned to work, learned to appreciate a dollar, which I didn't see too many of. I learned to appreciate what I had, which wasn't much. I learned from my experiences."

Massimino Santarelli agreed. He was one of the more fortunate miners who was eventually able to own his own home. After his son, Tom, finished high school, Massimino sold the house in order to pay for Tom's college education. "That," he said, "I couldn't have done in the old country."

The grown children of coal country are proud of their accomplishments as well as their sacrifices. Their stories are the legacy of coal country.

Bibliography and Acknowledgments

Aurand, Harold. *From the Molly Maguires to the United Mine Workers.*
Philadelphia, Pa.: Temple University Press, 1971.

———. "The Anthracite Strike: Its Social and Religious Effects." *Coal Towns:
A Contemporary Perspective, 1899–1923.* Edited by Harold Aurand.
Lexington, Mass.: Ginn Custom Publishing, 1980.

———. "Child Labor and the Welfare of Children in an Anthracite Coal-
Mining Town." *Coal Towns: A Contemporary Perspective, 1899–1923.*
Edited by Harold Aurand. Lexington, Mass.: Ginn Custom
Publishing, 1980.

———. "Do Your Duty! Editorial Response to the Anthracite Strike of 1902."
Hard Coal, Hard Times: Ethnicity and Labor in the Anthracite Region. Edited
by David L. Salay. Scranton, Pa.: Anthracite Museum Press, 1984.

Aurand, Harold, ed. *Coal Towns: A Contemporary Perspective, 1899–1923.*
Lexington, Mass.: Ginn Custom Publishing, 1980.

Benson, Ronald M. "Commentary: The Family Economy and Labor
Protest in Industrial America and the Coal and Iron Police in
Anthracite Country." *Hard Coal, Hard Times: Ethnicity and Labor in
Anthracite Region.* Edited by David L. Salay. Scranton, Pa.: Anthracite
Museum Press, 1984.

Blatz, Perry. "The All-Too-Youthful Proletarians," *Pennsylvania Heritage,*
Winter, 1981.

Bodner, John. *Anthracite People: Families, Unions, and Work, 1900–1940.* Harrisburg: Pennsylvania Historical and Museum Commission, 1983.

———. "The Family Economy and Labor Protest in Industrial America:
Hard Coal Miners in the 1930s." *Hard Coal, Hard Times: Ethnicity and
Labor in Anthracite Region.* Edited by David L. Salay. Scranton, Pa.:
Anthracite Museum Press, 1984.

123

Brestensky, Dennis, Evelyn A. Hovanec, and Albert N. Skomra. *Patch/Work Voices: The Culture and Lore of a Mining People*. Pittsburgh, Pa.: University of Pittsburgh Press, 1991.

Carter, Goodrich. *The Miner's Freedom*. New York: Arno Press, 1977.

Couch, Stephen R. "The Coal and Iron Police in Anthracite Country." *Hard Coal, Hard Times: Ethnicity and Labor in Anthracite Region*. Edited by David L. Salay. Scranton, Pa.: Anthracite Museum Press, 1984.

Fallows, Alice K. "A Woman's Visit to the Coal Fields." *Outlook*. October 11, 1902.

Hambridge, Jay. "An Artist's Impression of the Colliery Region." *Coal Towns: A Contemporary Perspective, 1899–1923*. Edited by Harold Aurand. Lexington, Mass.: Ginn Custom Publishing, 1980.

Handlin, Oscar. *The Uprooted: The Epic Story of the Great Migrations That Made the American People*. Boston: Little, Brown and Co., 1973.

Korson, George. *Black Rock: Mining Folklore of the Pennsylvania Dutch*. Baltimore: Johns Hopkins University Press, 1960.

———. *Minstrels of the Mine Patch: Songs and Stories of the Anthracite Industry*. Hatboro, Pa.: Folklore Associates, Inc., 1964.

Kraus, Corrine Azen. *Grandmothers, Mothers, and Their Daughters: Oral Histories of Three Generations of Ethnic American Women*. Boston: Twayne Publishers, 1991.

Lantz, Herman R., with J. S. McCrary. *People of Coal Town*. New York: Columbia University Press, 1958.

MacLean, Annie Marion. "Life in the Pennsylvania Coal Fields with Particular Reference to Women." *Coal Towns: A Contemporary Perspective, 1899–1923*. Edited by Harold Aurand. Lexington, Mass.: Ginn Custom Publishing, 1980.

McKeever, Eric. *Tales of the Mine Country*. 8506 Valleyfield Road, Lutherville, Md. 21903.

Miller, Donald L., and Richard E. Sharpless. *The Kingdom of Coal: Work, Enterprise, and Ethnic Communities in the Mine Fields.* Philadelphia: University of Pennsylvania Press, 1985.

Nichols, Francis H. "Children of the Coal Shadow." *Coal Towns: A Contemporary Perspective, 1899–1923.* Edited by Harold Aurand. Lexington, Mass.: Ginn Custom Publishing, 1980.

Norris, Frank. "Life in the Mining Region: A Study in Strike-Time Conditions of Living in Representative Mining Towns." *Everybody's Magazine.* September 7, 1902.

Poliniak, Louis. *When Coal Was King: Mining Pennsylvania's Anthracite.* Lebanon, Pa.: Applied Arts Publishers, 1970.

Report of the Department of Mines of Pennsylvania: Anthracite Region, 1903.

Report of the Inspectors of the Mines, 1870.

Roberts, Ellis. *The Breaker Whistle Blows.* Scranton, Pa.: Anthracite Museum Press, 1987.

Roberts, Peter. *Anthracite Coal Communities: A Study of the Demography of the Anthracite Regions.* New York: Macmillan Co., 1904.

Rood, Henry Edward. "A Pennsylvania Colliery Village." *Coal Towns: A Contemporary Perspective, 1899–1923.* Edited by Harold Aurand. Lexington, Mass.: Ginn Custom Publishing, 1980.

Roy, Andrew Hon. *A History of the Coal Miners of the United States: From the Development of the Mines to the Close of the Anthracite Strike of 1902.* Ohio: J. L. Trauger Printing Co., 1933.

Scranton Republican. June 29, 30, July 1, 2, 1896; June 6, 1919.

Seltzer, Curtis. *Fire in the Hole: Miners and Managers in the American Coal Industry.* Lexington: University Press of Kentucky, 1983.

Shopes, Linda. "Oral History in Pennsylvania: A Historiographic Overview." *Pennsylvania History.* vol. 60, no. 4, October 1993.

Wallace, Andrew F. C. "The Miners of St. Claire: Family, Class, and Ethnicity in a Mining Town in Schuylkill County, 1850–1880." *Hard Coal, Hard Times: Ethnicity and Labor in Anthracite Region.* Edited by David L. Salay. Scranton, Pa.: Anthracite Museum Press, 1984.

Works Progress Administration, Federal Writers' Project, Job No. 54, Record Group 11, 12, 13, 14. The project is located in the Bureau of Archives and History, Pennsylvania Historical and Museum Commission, Harrisburg, Pa.

Personal Interviews: Carlo Brunori, Anna Cardoni, Emil Ermert, Mary Fanucci, Lil Ferretti, Marie Hoban, Joe Mickatavage, Victor Mickatavage, Richard Owens, Massimino Santarelli, Pearl Santarelli, Gabriella Slivinski, Leo Sliviniski, Howard Smith, John Sutkowsky, Samuel Wentovich.

Additional resources include interview tapes and transcripts located at Eckley Village (Joe Charnigo, Helen Fedorsha, Bruno Lagonosky, Mary Marshlik) and the Bureau of Archives and History at the Pennsylvania Historical and Museum Commission in Harrisburg (Joe Boley, William Jones, Joseph McCormick, William McKinney, Alex McLaughlin, Patrick McNulty, Joseph Miliauskas, Thomas Miller, Joseph O'Boyle, William O'Boyle, Stephen O'Boyle, Robert Reid, Jack Stanton, James Sullivan, Ferdinand Woll, and several anonymous interviewees).

This project could not have been completed without the support of the following people and institutions: my writers' group—Lisa Rowe Fraustino, Norma DeNault Grula, Mary Joyce Love, Elaine Slivinski Lisandrelli, Laura Lee Wren, Clara Gillow Clark Varrichio; my museum contacts—Chester Kulesa (Scranton Anthracite Heritage Museum), Lance Metz (Canal Museum at Hugh Moore Park), Leo Ward (Schuylkill County Historical Society), Cynthia Chapman (Wyoming Historical and Geological Society); my "slide" expert, Joe Sadowski; my postcard contacts, Jack Hiddlestone and Charlie Kumpas; all the people who allowed me into their homes to conduct interviews; my agent, Barrie Van Dyck; my editor, Karen Klockner; and, most of all, my family—Joe, Brandy, and Joey.